"I've seen Natasha's audiences burst into laughter, cheers, and applause at her verse. She captures the double standards, the dual ambitions, the ambiguities and worries, and, above all, the hopes and aspirations that are so much a part of modern women's lives, and she captures it all with marvelous humor."

—JUDY MANN,
The Washington Post

D0064278

IS
THIS
WHERE
I WAS
GOING?

·

NATASHA JOSEFOWITZ

Illustrated by
Françoise Gilot

Warner Books
A Warner Communications Company

Some of the poems in this volume have
appeared in the following books:

Paths to Power: A Woman's Guide from First Job to Top Executive
published by Addison-Wesley Publishing Company.
Copyright © 1980 by Natasha Josefowitz.

In a Nutshell published by Prestwick Publishing Co.
Copyright © 1982 by Natasha Josefowitz.

Copyright © 1983 by Natasha Josefowitz
Illustrations copyright © 1983 by Françoise Gilot
All rights reserved.
Warner Books, 666 Fifth Avenue, New York, NY 10103

W A Warner Communications Company

Printed in the United States of America
First printing: September 1983
10 9 8 7 6 5 4 3 2 1

Designed by Giorgetta Bell McRee

Library of Congress Cataloging in Publication Data

Josefowitz, Natasha.
Is this where I was going?

I. Title.
PS3560.O76I8   1983   811'.54   83-10415
ISBN 0-446-37580-2 (USA)
ISBN 0-446-37923-9 (Canada)

ATTENTION: SCHOOLS AND CORPORATIONS

Warner books are available at quantity discounts with bulk purchase for educational, business, or sales promotional use. For information, please write to: **Special Sales Department, Warner Books, 666 Fifth Avenue, New York, NY 10103.**

ARE THERE WARNER BOOKS YOU WANT
BUT CANNOT FIND IN YOUR LOCAL STORES?

You can get any **Warner Books** title in print. Simply send title and retail price, plus 75¢ per order and 50¢ per copy to cover mailing and handling costs for each book desired. New York State and California residents, add applicable sales tax. Enclose check or money order—no cash, please—to: **Warner Books, PO Box 690, New York, NY 10019. Or send for our complete catalog of Warner Books.**

To my mother . . .
always there

CONTENTS

PART ONE • At Work

PART TWO • At Home

PART THREE • With Men

PART FIVE • In Today's World

ACKNOWLEDGMENTS

I want to thank Fredda Isaacson, Senior Editor at Warner Books, not only for believing in this book and sorting through a couple of hundred poems, but also for her own poetic flair, which makes her a joy to work with. My appreciation goes also to Margaret McBride for her help and support.

I also want to thank Herman Gadon, who listened to many drafts, often willing to be interrupted in the midst of his own writing because "I just couldn't wait to read my latest one." His patience, devotion, and willingness to say "This one doesn't work" or "I love that one" helped shape this volume.

And, finally, my thanks to the women and men who wrote to me, saying that they had cut out my poems from magazines, taped them to office walls, or sent them to friends. Because of their letters, I know that we are sharing a common experience that needs to be expressed in ways everyone can recognize with a nod or a smile.

PART
ONE

•

At Work

—————

I Have Arrived

I have not seen the plays in town
    only the computer printouts
I have not read the latest books
    only *The Wall Street Journal*
I have not heard birds sing this year
    only the ringing of phones
I have not taken a walk anywhere
    but from the parking lot to my office
I have not shared a feeling in years
    but my thoughts are known to all
I have not listened to my own needs
    but what I want I get
I have not shed a tear in ages
    I have arrived
Is *this* where I was going?

Today's Women

We are
Today's women
Born yesterday
Dealing with tomorrow.

Good Management Potential

If I'm assertive,
I'm seen as aggressive.
If I'm aggressive,
I'm a bitch.
I won't be promoted.

Let's try it again.
   If I'm nonassertive,
   I'm seen as a patsy.
   If I'm a patsy,
   I won't be promoted.

Let's try it once more.
   If I'm very careful,
   I can go unnoticed.
   If I'm unnoticed,
   no one will know
   I want to be promoted.

Any suggestions?

Impressions from an Office

The family picture is on HIS desk.
Ah, a solid, responsible family man.

The family picture is on HER desk.
Umm, her family will come before her career.

HIS desk is cluttered.
He's obviously a hard worker and a busy man.

HER desk is cluttered.
She's obviously a disorganized scatterbrain.

HE is talking with his co-workers.
He must be discussing the latest deal.

SHE is talking with her co-workers.
She must be gossiping.

HE'S not at his desk.
He must be at a meeting.

SHE'S not at her desk.
She must be in the ladies' room.

HE'S not in the office.
He's meeting customers.

SHE'S not in the office.
She must be out shopping.

HE'S having lunch with the boss.
He's on his way up.

SHE'S having lunch with the boss.
They must be having an affair.

The boss criticized HIM.
He'll improve his performance.

The boss criticized HER.
She'll be very upset.

HE got an unfair deal.
Did he get angry?

SHE got an unfair deal.
Did she cry?

HE'S getting married.
He'll get more settled.

SHE'S getting married.
She'll get pregnant and leave.

HE'S having a baby.
He'll need a raise.

SHE'S having a baby.
She'll cost the company money in maternity benefits.

HE'S going on a business trip.
It's good for his career.

SHE'S going on a business trip.
What does her husband say?

HE'S leaving for a better job.
He knows how to recognize a good opportunity.

SHE'S leaving for a better job.
Women are not dependable.

Did I Sound OK?

Fifty people at the meeting—
I want to say something,
but is it relevant,
and is it pertinent?
And, is this the time?
Or should I wait?
Perhaps it is dumb.
Or has it been said?
I wish it were not so important
for me to sound clever
and original
whenever I talk,
wanting every time
to make an important contribution
to the goings-on.
I hate wanting others
to respect me.
I hate caring so much
that I should be liked.
Why should it matter?
But it does,
damn it, it *does*!
So with pounding heart
I say it—

Was it OK?
Tell me—how did I sound?

Stereotypes

She said to him,
"The academic life must be pleasant
You're a professor, how nice!"
He said to her,
"Well, maybe someday
you'll marry one"
She said to him,
"Why should I marry one
when I can be one?"

The Interview

—Are you married?
—Well, yes.
—And do you have children?
—No—no we don't.
—Aren't you planning to?
  After all, you're a young woman!
—No, we're not planning children now.
—Well, even if you're not planning, they'll come, and we
  would have trained you for nothing. . . .
—No, we're not planning children, and I'm very
  committed to a career.
—What methods of contraception do you use?

—What methods does your company
  suggest to its employees?

Promotion

If she wants to move up
but he wants to move in,
one of them will move out
and it won't be him.

Sexual Harassment at Work

This is my assistant.
She's a great girl.

I'm a woman, not a girl.

Look at her legs.
Hey, cutie!
What are you doing tonight?

I'm busy.

How about a little hug
so I can feel those lovely breasts.
My wife is a cold fish,
and a man needs some affection.

Please stop.

If you come across, honey,
I could do a lot for you.

I don't have affairs
with people I work with.

Oh, come on, don't be a prude.
I'll give you a real good time.

Really, I'm not interested.

What's the matter, sweetheart.
You're playing hard to get.
I know you want it.

You're wrong, leave me alone.

I know a horny little ass
when I see one.

Sigh.

Let me feel it just a bit.

Ouch!

Oh, that didn't hurt.
You like it.

Slap!

12

OK, if that's how you treat
a man who wants to help you in
your career, you're fired.

> But I do the job well and
> I need the money.

Then, if you know what's good
for you, you'll take those
panties off right now.

. . . . .

Can't Do It All!

If I do this
I won't get that done
If I do that
this will slip by
If I do both
neither will be perfect.

Not everything worth doing
is worth doing well.

Gone Are the Good Old Days

When I patted her back
as I passed by her desk,
she used to smile.
Now she says,
"Don't touch me."

When I put my arm around her
and introduced her as "my girl,"
she used to thank me.
Now she says,
"I'm not your girl."

When I pinched her behind
as she leaned over to file,
she used to giggle.
Now she says,
"You are harassing me."

When I told her how I scored last night,
she used to laugh.
Now she says,
"I don't want to hear about it."

When I lied to my wife
about having to work late,
she used to cover for me.
Now she refuses.

When I asked her to do my shopping,
she used to be delighted.
Now she says,
"It's not in my job description."

She Who Gets Hired

She who gets hired
is not necessarily the one
who can do that job best,
but the one who knows
the most about
how to get hired.

Feminine Wiles Don't Seem to Work

If all women get hired
because of affirmative action
and all get promoted
because they slept with the boss,
why are we still
in only 6% of middle management positions
and less than 1% in top executive ones?

That's How It Is

Most men are assumed competent
   until proven otherwise.
Most women are assumed incompetent
   unless proven otherwise.

If Sex Is Seen As Possible,
Sex Is Seen As Probable

If he greets her warmly
he must have a crush

If she smiles at him
she's flirting

If she goes to his office
she has ulterior motives

If she's in there too long
God knows what they're doing

If he closes the door
we know what's going on

If they work late together
do their spouses know?

If they're having lunch
they're having an affair

And if they don't . . .
they must have broken up.

Dual Career Family

When he brings home the bacon,
she fries it.

When she brings home the bacon, too,
they eat out.

Office Politics

Knowing the difference between:
what people *say* they want
and what they really *want*
and do not say

The New Double Binds

We're damned if we do—
damned if we don't,
I'm either screwing up
or being screwed.

If I'm home with the kids,
I'm not liberated,
if I go to work,
I'm a bad mother.

I either don't do enough for my husband,
according to his mother,
or I do too much,
according to mine.

If I'm too pretty,
I won't get hired
because I'll distract the men.
If I'm too plain,
I won't get hired.
Who wants unattractive females around?

If I wear my three-piece suit,
I look too mannish,
if I wear a dress,
I'm not professional.

If I bring in the coffee,
that's all I'm good for,
if I don't,
I'm one of those women's-libbers.

If I eat lunch with my boss,
the secretaries gossip,
if I eat with the secretaries,
I'm seen as "just one of the girls."

If I don't work overtime—
women want special considerations,
if I do,
I'm a rate-buster.

If I ask her to retype a letter—
women bosses are bitches,
if I don't,
I have no standards.

If I agree,
I have no opinions,
if I disagree,
I'm aggressive.

If I smile,
I'm seductive,
if I don't,
I'm cold.

If I stop this list here,
I haven't said enough,
if I don't,
it will get too long.

So damned if we don't
and still damned if we do,
I'll just be like me
and you be like you.

"F" Is for Female

Name
Address
Occupation
and two boxes
"Please check one"
If I check "M" would I have a better chance?
If I said male
would I get the job?
I'll never know
because
I checked the box marked "F."

Leadership

If the best of me can make more of you,
then the best of you will reflect on me.

PART TWO

•

At Home

Occupation: Housewife

"What do you do?"
—"Nothing,
I'm just a housewife."
"What do you do as a housewife?"
—"Nothing,
I have two children,
so I market,
cook three meals a day,
clean, do the wash, mend,
dust, vacuum,
take the children
to school, the dentist, music lessons,
buy them shoes,
bandage a knee,
repair a bike,
pay bills,
put away toys,
read stories,
market,
cook three meals a day,
clean, do the wash, mend,
dust, vacuum.
Nothing."

Floor Scrubbing

The 20's

He's a student.   She's a student.

They both scrub the floors.

The 30's

He gets a job.   She gets a baby.

She scrubs the floors.

He sometimes helps.

The 40's

He gets promoted.   She gets a job.

She scrubs the floors.

The 50's

He gets a presidency.   She gets a maid.

The maid scrubs the floors.

The 60's

He retires.   She gets promoted.

He scrubs the floors.

Tribal Talk

or

Women Are the Bearers of the Oral Traditions of Our Culture

I use three egg yolks . . .
When my three-year-old was jealous of the baby . . .
This dressmaker charges only . . .
A good cream for rashes . . .
The best thing for morning sickness . . .
There's a good sale at . . .
With a colicky baby . . .
When my mother-in-law visits . . .
I read this book on adolescents . . .
Caffeine is bad for you . . .
I plant in late Spring . . .
There is more protein in . . .
The funniest movie . . .
I lost five pounds by just . . .
When I'm too exhausted to . . .
I'll try it . . .
When my children . . .
How did you . . .
Me, too.
You're not alone.

The Executive's Wife

Company for dinner . . .
his business associates,
hors d'oeuvres,
hot and cold.
Be sure to have
enough liquor in the house,
enough soda,
dress attractively,
but not too.
House should be clean,
children out of the way.
Greet them smiling,
chitchat.
Don't talk business.
If they do,
they'll apologize
for being boring.
"I don't mind—
in fact I'm interested."
Polite smiles,
nice home,
lovely dinner,
well brought-up children,
becoming dress,
charming wife.
Oh, thank you,
thank you for your favorable comments
on the house,
   the dinner,
   the children,
   the dress,

the wife
(in that order?)
It was a *huge* success!

So why did the charming wife
    in her becoming dress
    with the well brought-up children
    and the lovely dinner
    in the nice home . . .
    Leave?

Time Out

A gray day in November,
too warm for a chimney fire
too cold to go out.

Too much work to play
but not quite enough
to preclude daydreaming.

A hot cup of tea
with a lemon slice,
a spoon of brown sugar,
a clove, a nutmeg,
a cinnamon stick,
and just a little bit of rum.

Ah—

The New Nightgown

Pink with ruffles
and pretty ribbons,
a touch transparent.
No one to see me
looking so lovely.
What a waste!

Why Not?

Sometimes confident
Sometimes scared
Sometimes in charge
Sometimes dependent
Sometimes tigress
Sometimes lamb
Sometimes Mother Goose
Sometimes Goldilocks
Wanting to be assertive
afraid of the consequences
Wanting to be feminine
afraid of the powerlessness
Wanting male prerogatives
afraid to compete for them
Wanting my cake
and to eat it, too.

Well, why not?

Willpower

I have willpower
for everything
except for what's fattening
Comes food
and I can't resist
I will wait five minutes
talking to myself
then eat it anyway—
and even take second helpings
Kicking myself all along
for having no willpower
Help!

The Roses in My Garden

The roses in my garden
are more beautiful,
more fragrant,
and give me more pleasure
than any I can buy in a store.

And so it is with my children,
who are smarter than all others
and with my exquisite taste in art
and with my great life-style.

Unless, of course,
it is the opposite—
and my roses are really runty,
and my children not so terrific,
and my taste is unsure,
and my life-style is for the birds.

None of which
has to do with reality
but with the way
I feel today.

Traveling in My Kitchen

French fries
English muffins
Danish pastry
Turkish delights
Russian borscht
Greek salad
Italian sausage
Swiss cheese
Belgian endive
German kraut
Chinese cabbage
Mideastern pita bread
Nova Scotia salmon
New York cheesecake
Boston lettuce

Dutch treat

I'm Not OK, You're Not OK, but That's OK

I have done bad things in my life
have had bad thoughts
I am not always kind
nor always generous
I have placed myself first
I have lied, cheated,
I have acted out of passion
which has hurt others.
I have been inconsiderate
punishing, even vengeful
and I have felt guilty
tried to make amends
tried to atone
made New Year's resolutions
about becoming better.

I know some very similar things about you.

So I'm not OK
and you're not OK;
but that's OK.

Thin Tricks

If I take many small slivers of cake
instead of one large slice,
I am really eating less.
If I keep evening out
the uneven edges of the pie,
I'm not really eating it.
If I eat off your plate,
I'm not eating off mine.
If I finish the children's leftovers,
it doesn't count.
If I don't order a meal,
but taste everyone else's,
I won't gain weight.
So how come
I'm not thin?

What Am I?*

Somewhere between always giving to others
and always keeping it all to myself,
I stand.
Somehow between only caring for others
and only caring for me,
I live.
But when I am only for others,
I ask,
"Who will be for me?
And when I am only for me,
then what am I?"

*Adapted from Hillel, Aboth 1:14, The Talmud of Babylon.

The Cookie Exchange

"Please bring three dozen cookies
and your recipe,"
said the invitation.
Oh, horrors!
How can I admit
I never baked a cookie
in my life?
I call a friend
who has a daughter
who has a recipe
that is really easy—
and so I do it.
They turn out
big, thick, and gloppy.
Everyone else's
are petits fours—small and dainty.
I am ashamed
until the kids come in
and say,
"Oh, goody,
real cookies!"
And eat mine up first.

Remorse and Regret

Is it better to have
remorse than regret?
Remorse is for what you did
and wish you hadn't.
Regret is for what you did not do
and wish you had.

I have always preferred
sins of commission
over those of omission,
thinking that action
is better than nonaction;
when, in fact,
not to act
is also a decision
and as real a choice.

Daily Dilemmas

If I take a soft drink,
I get the sugar,
calories, and cavities.

If I drink Lo-Cal,
I get saccharin or cyclamates
and a chance at cancer.

I'm not always sure
whether I'd rather
die young but thin
or old and fat.

Exercise

Any excuse not to do it . . .
A slight morning backache
is a welcome impediment
The usual one is
"No time now, I'm late already"
Although I feel better all day
if I exercise in the morning
I manage not to
and luxuriate in bed
feeling deliciously guilty
Another fifteen minutes
Really believing that
"I'll start tomorrow for sure."

TV

Sometimes in the evening
I'm so tired
I can't read,
I can't write,
I can't talk,
I can't think,
and it's too early
to go to sleep.
So I watch TV
sitting in bed,
but I still
feel guilty
that I'm not
being constructive
(whatever that is).
But where is it written
that it's not OK
to waste time?
And, anyway,
what's wasted time?
If I enjoy it,
then it's not wasted.

Unafraid

If I am small and weak,
then I act big and strong
lest I be found out
and not be loved.

When I am big and strong,
then I can ask for help—
unafraid of what they will think,
Unafraid to seem weak,
Unafraid.

The Box of Chocolates

My favorite kind . . .
truffles with nuts.
Where can I put them
so that I'm not tempted?
Nowhere.
All day I think of them . . .
visualizing the neat brown rows,
tasting the indescribable flavor.
If I eat one,
I'll eat two.
No, three, four, the box.
It's easy.
As soon as I'm finished
I will hate myself for hours.
It's either obsession with deprivation
or gluttony with guilt.
Next time
please bring me flowers.

Something Nice Happened

I'm so excited
I can't sleep.
When I don't sleep,
I get exhausted.
When I'm exhausted,
I can't work.
When I don't work,
I feel guilty.
When I feel guilty,
I get anxious.
When I'm anxious,
I can't sleep!

Friendship

She served
warm Brie with almonds,
then a veal stew,
a salad,
and baked a grand dessert.
The children went to bed
without fussing.
We drank good wine,
sat by the fire,
talked about life,
and felt blessed
to have such good friends.

Needlepoint

In . . . out
In . . . out
With every stitch
a new pinpoint of color.
From a piece of canvas
and a bit of wool
a design emerges
as I go in . . . out,
each color, each line
the precursor of a new stitch,
the sum so much larger
than any of its parts.
My needle has a life of its own,
seeming to know where to go next,
and I must be very attentive
to follow its imperatives
as well as my own,
so that together
we can create
something even lovelier
than what I had imagined alone.

Please Fix the Toaster, Dear

The toaster did not work.
He promised to fix it
but he didn't.

I put the bread
under the broiler.
When I took it out
I burned my hand
badly
against the coils.

He fixed the toaster.

PART
THREE
•
With Men

Thou

A loaf of bread,
a jug of wine,
and thou . . .
In that order?

I'd rather
have "thou" first
and eat later.

Patterns

Instead of minimizing our differences,
let us maximize them
Instead of denying that you are better at this
and I am better at that,
let us take full advantage of our special skills
and recognize the weaknesses
in order either to work on them
or turn to what we do best
It is OK with me
that most men have better spatial skills
and that most women are better at verbal skills
I can accept that most men are more concerned with
    objects
and most women with people
That boys excel at gross motor coordination
and girls at manual dexterity
That males are good at problem-solving
and females process information faster
I like our differences!
As you shovel the driveway
I fix you hot soup
As you drive at night
I keep you awake
As you carry the suitcases
I check in at the counter
You figure our taxes
I decide on our budget
You vacuum
I dust
You turn the mattress over
I water the plants

You chop the onions
I add the spices
You go marketing . . .
but with my shopping list
You buy me books
I buy you ties
You know how to cure the ills of the world
I know how to cure your ills
You know what the children ought to do
I know how they are
You know about driving in the snow
I know you should wear a scarf
You show me how much you love me
I tell it to you
I could not do well what you do so well
nor could you do what I do
I like me as me
and you as you.

The Gift

He bought me an expensive present
He was so pleased
The size is just right
He went to five stores to find it
Except I don't like it—
it just isn't my taste
If I exchange it
he'll be offended
If I don't
I'll wear it
only once or twice
to please him
I hate the waste
but even more
I hate
not knowing
what to do.

Priorities

We're working too hard
accomplishing a lot but . . .
the time to play is passing us by.

We're in our separate worlds
of creative concentration
It's wonderful but . . .
the time to be is passing us by.

We meet for meals
and speak of work
It's helpful but . . .
the time to know is passing us by.

We meet in bed
and go to sleep
It's restful but . . .
the time to love is passing us by.

Waiting

He's late.
It's dark.
Supper is ready.
He usually calls.
I can't read
—too anxious.
Passing headlights
reflect in my window.
I jump—
it's him!
No.
Maybe a car accident,
a heart attack,
a stroke,
maybe he fell.
He has an ID on him—
they would call me.
Do they call right away?
Who calls?
The police, the doctors?
Do they come personally
if it's terrible news?
The phone rings,
I startle—
it's him!
No.
I do my needlepoint.
Maybe it's the last happy minute of my life
because I don't know yet,
don't know the awful news.
I will say afterward,

"I had this premonition."
I'm hungry.
Shall I eat without him?
I better eat now.
In case of bad news,
I won't be able to later . . .
Oh, God,
I can't stand it.
I hear the garage door—
it's him!
Yes!!!

He had met this friend
and you know how it is . . .

Questions

When you say,
"I love you,"
I say right back,
"I love you, too."
And when I say,
"I love you,"
and you say nothing,
though I know you do,
I sit up and ask,
"Don't you love me, too?"

Connections

Your allowing me to know you
has permitted me to be known.
Thank you.

When I'm Fully in Charge of Me

When I'm fully in charge of me,
   I can let you, too, be free.

When I am using my fullest potential,
   I can help others do the same.

When I am empowered and strong and sure,
   I feel neither envious nor threatened.

When I can grow at my own rate,
   I do not fear your taking anything away.

I do not fear your overtaking me.

May I Introduce You To

my friend
uh . . .
my great and good friend
my boyfriend
my man
my colleague
my beau
my mate.
Well . . .
my roommate
my lover
my beloved
my sweetie
my sex object.
Ha-ha . . .
my fiancé
my full-time equivalent
my significant other.
You see, it's like this . . .
he's my friend
and I . . .
and he . . .
and we . . .

He Does Not Know

He does not know
I'm watching him
standing in the bathtub
I like his body
He's soaping himself
automatically
lost in his thoughts
He has narrow hips
and a tender ass
a long thin torso
with a well-shaped head
full of thick hair
and a beautiful face
with loving blue eyes
He stands very straight
and looks great in clothes—
but I like him naked.
He feels more mine.

Chicken Soup

When I have a cold
a sore throat
a slight fever
on weekdays
I go to work anyway.
But on a Sunday,
I stay in bed
feeling sorry for myself
coughing and sneezing
and complaining.
He sits at the foot
of my bed
with a look of concern.
"Tea," he offers,
or perhaps juice.
He smiles reassuringly,
"I'm sorry you're so sick.
Shall I rub your neck?"
I sigh, I mumble, I groan,
but it's all worth it
just to have him sit
at the foot of my bed
looking at me
so lovingly.

Fantasy at a Party

Too many people.
I sit alone.
My *eye* catches his.
What a good-looking man!
He smiles.
I smile back.
He comes over
a bit tentatively
and asks shyly
if he can sit next to me.
"Please do," I say.
He's a doctor
or writer
or doing some fascinating research,
and we find mutual friends,
shared interests.
We like the same books.
He knows about music and art.
Well-traveled
and independently wealthy.
Single, of course.
He touches my hand.
Shivers run down my spine.
The chemistry is right.
Electricity's in the air.
I am filled with happiness
and excitement.
I am alive,
tingling,
this is it—
Why doesn't he ever
Come to the same parties I do?

Dining Alone in a Restaurant

"Will you be dining alone?"
asks the maître d'.
"Yes," I reply.
He frowns disapprovingly . . .
I get to sit
near the kitchen door.
"These empty tables
are all reserved,"
I am told.
I sit self-consciously
wishing I had dined in my room.
Then "he" walks in
handsome, well-dressed, at ease.
He notices me
calls the waiter over.
He's ordering me
a glass of wine.
No, a bottle of champagne.
He didn't . . .
oh, well!
He's writing something
a note
to ask if he can join me.
He didn't . . .
oh, well!
He gets up.
He will come over
and say,
"You are irresistible.
I am smitten.
Let us go dancing together."
He didn't . . .
Oh, well!

Ritual

Dim awareness.
I'm waking up;
he stirs, too.
We hug
and mumble,
"How did you sleep?"
A question
not requiring
an answer.
He turns the heat on in the house.
I turn on the radio.
We wait ten minutes
together in bed
sharing dreams,
analyzing them.
We exercise,
dancing
to fast music,
until out of breath—
so much for our cardiovascular systems.
I stretch,
he does push-ups.
Then he shaves,
I get breakfast,
which I bring to bed
on two trays.
The best time of the day is about to begin
to the sounds of our rushing stream
and with a view over our treetops
through which squirrels do gymnastics.

We have breakfast in bed:
tea,
sourdough whole wheat bread,
and goat cheese.
We try to eat slowly
to make the moment last.

If I could change only one thing in my life,
I would change my metabolism,
so that I could eat breakfast all day.

Territory*

Are you more if I'm less?
Do I breathe your air
or fly in your space?
When I take up more room,
do you become constrained?
Do you value me more
when I'm beholden to you?
Do you value me less
when I'm free and I soar?
Are you less if I'm more?

*Adapted from "Woman to Man" by J. R. Wells, August 1977.

Made for Each Other

He does his own thing
and she lets him

She does everything
and he lets her

The Trouble with Men

If he's turned on
because I'm pretty or fun,
and he makes a pass
and I turn him down,
he's angry
because he says
it's my fault
he's turned on.
And, therefore,
I'm expected
to come across,
when in fact
he turns himself on
using me.

I bear
no responsibility
and certainly
no guilt.

Trust

I don't know
What is best for you.
But I trust you to know that
I know
What is best for me.
And I trust you
To trust me.

The Boss's Secretary

He pats her on the head
He sees it as fatherly
She sees it as demeaning.

He tells her a dirty joke
He thinks it's funny
She thinks it's gross.

He says that she's cute
He thinks it's a compliment
She thinks, "I'm not his daughter."

He asks her to sew on a button
He thinks she'll be glad to
She thinks, "I'm not his mother."

He tells her to get him coffee
He thinks it's proper
She thinks, "I'm not his servant."

He makes a pass at her
He thinks she'll enjoy it
She thinks, "I'm not his sex object."

He asks her for a date
He thinks she will be flattered
She's afraid to refuse.

Unwritten Rules

When I was young
I used to flirt with older men
for the pleasure
of getting them a bit excited.
I felt safe
because they were older.
If they flirted back
and that was all,
they were playing the game correctly.
But if they took me seriously,
I became scared
because if I was a "cute-daughter-person,"
they were supposed to be "amused father."
But if they became sexual instead,
That was not part of the deal.
The game wasn't fun anymore.
They had turned into "dirty old men."

The New Etiquette

He hires her—
it is reverse discrimination,
He doesn't—
he's not complying with affirmative action.

He promotes her—
he's playing favorites,
He doesn't—
he's sexist.

He opens the door for her—
she doesn't need his help,
He does not open the door—
he's a boor.

He lights her cigarette—
he's old-fashioned,
He doesn't—
he's rude.

He picks up the dinner check—
she's offended,
He doesn't—
he's stingy.

He greets her with a kiss—
he's unprofessional,
He doesn't—
he's cold.

He gives her a raise—
he has ulterior motives,
He doesn't—
he's a bastard.

How Is a Man to Know?

Some women
say no
when they really mean yes.
They have been taught
to play hard to get.

Other women
say no
when they really mean no.

How is a man to know?

PART FOUR

•

With Our Families

Titles

My grandmother was a lady.
My mother is "one of the girls."
I am a woman.
My daughter is a doctor.

Accessibility

Father is taking a nap.
His door is closed.
Children tiptoe
and whisper,
"Shh, Father's asleep."

Mother is taking a nap.
Her door is open
so she can hear
children fight or cry.
Mothers never take
real naps.

Not Enough

"Hi, Mom
next week
I'll be in town
and stay for dinner
and spend the night."

—Why only one night?

My Mother Complains That:

I've gained weight,
my hair isn't right,
my dress is unbecoming,
I wasn't polite.

I should have expected
more from the children,
less from my husband.
I have the wrong friends,
a messy house,
cook too little,
work too hard,
should visit her more,
call more often.

It matters not
that she complains.
What matters
is that it still matters.

My Father

My father died
many years ago.
And yet when something special
happens to me,
I need to tell him about it.
I talk to him secretly
not really knowing
whether he hears,
but it makes me feel better
to half believe it.

The Displaced Homemaker

They ate the food I cooked for them.
They wore the clothes I washed.
They slept in the beds I made.
They spent money they did not earn.

I took them to their lessons,
drove them to visit their friends,
put their teeth in braces,
and enrolled them in summer camp.

I helped them with their homework,
told stories, taught them songs.
I insisted on good manners
and cried when things went wrong.

I listened to their problems,
settled their disputes,
nursed them when they sickened,
and cuddled them a lot.

Now they do not need me.
They're grown-ups, on their own.
I'm called "displaced homemaker"—
a label I disown,
for when they come to visit me,
they say they're "coming home."

Role Reversals

My mother is growing old
slowly.
Her walk less brisk,
her hair not tinted anymore
give her away.

She complains
of not sleeping well,
of not being able
to flatten her stomach
in spite of exercise.

She does not talk
of facelifts anymore
and often asks
to have things repeated.
Does she not hear
or does she not understand?

She, known as "the doctor"
in our family,
now asks advice of me.

Little by little,
I am becoming
my mother's
mother.

The People My Children Married

If my son
brings breakfast in bed
to my daughter-in-law,
she's a lazy good-for-nothing
and he spoils her.

If my son-in-law
brings breakfast in bed
to my daughter,
she deserves it
and he's a doll.

My Children Are Outgrowing Me

I have a daughter
who is a doctor.
She knows things
I do not know.

I have a son
who is a writer.
He writes of things
I didn't know he knew.

I am proud
and yet a bit dismayed
that my children
are outgrowing me.

The first shock
was when they grew taller.
The second
was when they grew smarter.
Will they someday also
grow older?

It's Always the Mother's Fault

If her son peddles drugs
and her daughter, her body . . .
If one child is too fat
and the other too skinny . . .
If he drops out of school
and she lives with a creep . . .
If he won't find a job
and she wears too much makeup . . .
If the kids are too hip
or too apathetic . . .
It's their mother's fault.

She should have been more strict
or perhaps more lenient . . .
She should have sent them to camp
or perhaps kept them home . . .
She expected too much
or perhaps not enough.

She should have had a curfew
or allowed independence . . .
She should have helped with homework
or left them on their own . . .
She should be more involved
but perhaps was too much so . . .
Kids should lead their own lives
but stay close to home.

If children do well,
it is all to their credit . . .
If they don't turn out right,
it's their mother's fault.

My Children Graduate

Twenty-two years at the same job
including evenings and weekends.
No vacation time to speak of,
and now it's done:
PROJECT SUCCESSFULLY COMPLETED!
Yet, no farewell party,
no inscribed medal,
not even a watch
to commemorate a full-time job
held for twenty-two years
with very little complaint.

There had been no grievance procedures,
no upward mobility,
no horizontal enrichment,
no lateral moves,
and the rewards were mostly vicarious.

While everyone is pleased,
no one is particularly grateful.
It is normal, it seems,
that while they get their pictures taken
I once more just do the applauding.

I Sound Just Like My Mother

Sometimes I sound just like my mother,
and I'm shocked
at what crosses my lips.
I used to think,
I'll never say things like that,
but now and then I do.

Sometimes I catch
a glimpse in the mirror,
and I'm shocked.
I look just like my mother.

Is this her immortality—
to continue to live through me?

My Daughter the Doctor

Two photos on my desk:
one of my son
holding his Harvard diploma
and one of my daughter
in her wedding dress.

She saw these pictures one day,
got very upset, and said,
"You're proud of your son's MBA
and of the fact that your daughter found a husband,
but my graduation picture is not on your desk.
Mother, you're sexist!"
She was right!

I now have a photo of her
holding her diploma, too,
next to still another one
of Nina, my daughter the doctor,
holding her baby.

Where Are the Children of Yesteryear?

Where is the infant
suckling at my breast?
I find no traces of her
in that other young mother.

Where is the little boy
who crept into my bed?
Is there anything left of him
in that balding young man?

Where are my children
at each of their birthdays?
I do not see them
in these tall adults.

How did my little ones
become these people
almost as old as I?

Where is the caterpillar
when it becomes butterfly
or the tadpole
when it grows into frog?

My little children
are no longer.
They live only
in old photographs.

Wouldn't it be wonderful
if all our children
from all their past birthdays
could visit with us
just once in a while!

To My Future Daughter-in-law

If you marry my son
you really ought to know . . .
he always leaves his underwear
lying on the floor
and does not have the slightest notion
of how it ends up
folded in a drawer.

He won't hang up
his clothes in the closet
so there is never a chair
you can sit on.
He doesn't make his bed,
talks on the phone for hours,
is always late for dates,
and goes to sleep too late.

He will not eat leftovers,
does not like paper plates,
he changes his mind often
for reasons no one knows.
He's obsessive, compulsive,
hardworking, great fun,
you'll never be bored
with my wonderful son.

So take good care of him.

The Russian Shawl

I bought myself in Russia
this huge black shawl
with large red flowers
which made me feel like a gypsy.
I loved it.

While I was away
he gave it to his daughter
he said it was a mistake
he felt very bad about it.

I'm glad his daughter has it.
I'm sorry that I do not.
I'm angry he gave it away.
I'm guilty that I'm angry.
I told him it's OK,
but it's not true.
So I lied to make him feel better
but lying makes me feel worse.
I would rather feel bad
than make him feel bad.

Does all that make me a good person after all?

I'm Getting to Be an Old Fuddy-duddy

Small children are visiting
they come in and immediately
make a dash for the pantry,
look through the fridge.
    Doesn't their mother feed them?

They eat in the living room,
crumbs on the floor,
jam on the couch.
    Can't they eat in the kitchen?

They open a package of cookies,
a new box of crackers,
when I have some laid out.
    Doesn't their mother notice?

They trample my flowers,
track dirt into the house,
spill milk on the rug.
    Can't their mother control them?

They tear up magazines
I haven't yet read,
fingerprint windowpanes.
    Don't they have any toys?

Then they whine and complain.
There is nothing to play with.
They want to go home.
    It's about time!

The Stepdaughter

Tension in the air,
unease,
I'm on my toes.
My stepdaughter is visiting.
I like her—
that's not the issue.
It's this tension in the air.
After all these years
we still test each other.
We evaluate.
We are judgmental.
Does it ever stop?
Will we someday
take each other for granted,
accept one another
as women of the same family?
I hope so,
but I don't know
how to make it happen
now.

Miracles

My daughter
has a daughter.

I have a granddaughter.

My mother is a great-grandmother.

All miracles.

First Grandchild

Over 3,000 miles away from me
there is a child in Canada,
a brand-new child.
And here in my solar plexus
there is this new joy
that is like an old pain
I recognize.

The vulnerability
of loving so much,
of caring so much,
of worrying about another person now
for the rest of my life.

I don't know her yet
but we are inextricably bound forever—
my new grandchild and I.

For Laura

Size one month, please,
with matching booties in pink and blue—
Laura's first dress.

A soft teddy bear, please,
with a music box inside—
Laura's first toy.

And a grandmother
far, far away is writing
Laura's first poem.

PART
FIVE
·
In Today's
World

Women's Liberation

We're not yet
where we're going;
but we're not still
where we were.

Tokens

The only woman at the meeting,
the only black in the group,
the older person with the young folk,
the homosexual,
the least educated,
the poorest,
the handicapped,
the only Jew,
the recently widowed.

Survival is in the finding of kindred spirits
anywhere.
Finding support in
the Women's Movement,
the Black Caucus,
the Grey Panthers,
the widow's group,
the gay community.

Finding support
where one can cry,
or explode,
or just be oneself
without representing
the women's point of view,
or the black culture,
or the Jewish people,
or the aged.

We need a place
not to be one down
but to be equal—
a place where we are *not* different
for a little time at least,
a place where we can trust the others,
a place where we don't fear
the sexists,
the racists,
the anti-Semites,
the elitists.
Where you don't have to be a couple to be invited out,
or straight,
or young and beautiful,
a place of our own
with a people of our own.

Just in order
to survive.

Sorcellery

For "knowledge"
you get acclaimed.
　Prizes—promotions.

For "knowing"
you get burned.
　Fantasies—fears.

"Knowledge" is a public fact,
up front.
You either have it or you don't,
and all can see.

"Knowing" is a private experience,
hidden.
If you know and don't tell,
it won't show.

White men in their heads
possess the Knowledge;
Women and Blacks, in their guts,
have the Knowing.

Warlocks, black men, black magic
weaving spells
witches, hags, fortune-tellers
casting curses!
Burn them all for their Knowing,
for their secret and fearful powers.
Only *Knowledge* will be
allowed here.

Teaching

Like an old amphora
I sit in the sands of time . . .
filled with the oil
of knowledge and experience.

Like freshly baked clay pots
they sit all around me . . .
filled with the pure waters
of youth and hope.

If I pour my oil too gently
into the water-filled pots,
it will stay on the surface . . .
each untouched by the other.

And so I vigorously shake
to make the two inseparable;
for only when the water becomes heavier with knowledge
can the oil become lighter with joy.

The Fifth Wheel

Why is it
that when a woman alone
is invited by a couple,
it's charity—
and she's grateful?
But when a man alone
is invited by a couple,
it's fun—
and he takes it for granted?

Why is it
that two women and one man
is one woman too many,
but two men and one woman
is a trio?

Is it because we assume
that if he is alone
it is out of choice?
And if she is alone
it is because
no one asked her.

Driving

He is constantly changing lanes
passing the slower drivers
muttering under his breath
as he weaves in and out
of traffic

I find myself a middle lane
that will take me
all the way to my destination
and drive contentedly behind
whoever happens to be in front
going at someone else's speed
just so that
I don't have to change lanes

He saves about ten minutes a day.
I save myself.

Room Service

Hello!
Room Service, please!
I wish to order breakfast:

Two poached eggs,
one underdone,
the other hard-boiled,
with one strip of limp bacon
and burnt toast.
Lukewarm coffee
with sour milk,
canned orange juice,
slightly fermented,
half spilt on the tray,
and make me wait about an hour, please.

—This is an unusual order,
not sure we can fill it.

—Of course you can;
you did yesterday.

He/She

He brags about her body.
She brags about his job.
He thinks she's cute.
She thinks he's strong.
He wants her to look pretty.
She wants him to sound intelligent.
He is proud of her running the house well.
She is proud of his position at work.
He repairs.
She mends.
He likes her deference.
She likes his dominance.
He admires her knowledge of the arts.
She admires his knowledge of politics.
He has the right answers.
She has the right questions.
He couldn't manage without her.
She couldn't manage without him.

Lately she's begun to wonder.

Notice

I notice
when all the *eye* contact
is between men—
excluding women.
I notice
when men address only each other.
I notice
when a woman speaks
it falls on deaf ears.
But later if a man
says the same thing,
it is heard as important.
Or what *she* said
is attributed to *him*.
I notice
that women are more often
interrupted by men
than the other way around.
That topics initiated by men
get more air time
than the ones generated by women.
When a woman speaks,
she represents the female point of view
and therefore is discounted,
for she speaks for all women—
not as an individual
but as a part of a category.
Yes—I notice,
    I hear,
    I *see*,
    and I hurt.

Sometimes I say something about it—
more often I don't.
Either way it is difficult.
And just as men don't notice
all this about women,
white people don't notice
these same things about people of color.
What I need to learn is to notice
not only when I am being discriminated against,
but when you, my black, Hispanic,
Asian friends and colleagues
are being treated that same way—
maybe even by me.

Nuclear Arms

Keeping "them" scared
keeps us scared.
Is that the way
we want to live?

Neither Cain nor Abel

I am my
sister's
keeper!

I AM MY
SISTER'S
KEEPER!

Stop the Clock, I Need a Rest

Just one day please
without the hour hand
making full circles.

One hour please
without the minutes
ticking by.

One minute then
for time to stop
so I can take a breather,
not look at my watch
and scream,
"I'm late again."

Christmas Holiday

I did it again.
The wrong resort.
I tried to save money,
all prepaid, of course.
It's not south enough,
the water is too cold,
the waves are too high,
the pool is too small,
the beach is crowded,
not much sun,
and I'm unhappy
dreaming of warm lagoons
where I'm not.
So
I walk around town,
sit in my room, and
read about places I'd rather be.

Support Systems

My right hand is being held
by someone who knows *more* than I,
and I am learning.
My left hand is being held
by someone who knows *less* than I,
and I am teaching.
Both my hands need thus be held
for me—to be.

War?

More arms
  just in case . . .
Nuclear arms
  just in case *they,* too . . .
Arms race
  must stay ahead
  to keep *them* from starting . . .
  each nation sitting
  on its stockpiles
  waiting for the other
  to make one false move.
Who decides
  what's a false move?

Changing Wardrobe

I don't wear sleeveless anymore—
new trembling skin under my arms.
I buy bathing suits with skirts
to hide my less-firm thighs.

No low-cut backs for me anymore—
two strange pleats under my shoulder blades.
No low-cut front either with pushed-up breasts—
they're not quite smooth enough.

I used to have red hair
and wore yellow, beige, and green.
Now that my hair is gray
I can wear bright reds and hot pinks
and look absolutely smashing.

It's Not the Wrinkles It's the Sag

It's not the crow's-feet
around my eyes.
I find these rather charming.
It's the puffiness below
and the extra skin on the eyelids.

It's not the deep furrows
on my forehead.
They make me look intelligent,
but the folds
around my mouth
change the contour of my jaw.

It's not the wrinkles
on my neck
but that funny piece of flesh
that hangs under my chin.

I place my hands
upon my temples,
pull back, saying,
"See, this is how I would look
with a facelift."
And a face ten years younger appears,
but it's not mine.
Then I let go
and smile at the familiar one.
Wrinkles, sag, and all,
knowing that's me
trying to age
Gracefully.

Plums and Prunes

Your skins are taut.
Your faces smooth
   like fresh plums.

My skin is wrinkled.
My brow furrowed
   like a prune.

Prunes are sweeter.

Born Yesterday

We have moved.
New neighborhood,
new job,
new friends.

We must create a history
so that we can have a past.
With every move
we are born yesterday,
all over again
with no shared memories.

I want to push the time
to bridge the gaps—
knowing others,
being known by them.
I want instant friendship,
instant love, care, trust.

I want in the new place
all I have lost in the old
without going through the rites of passage—
hoping to be accepted
without trying so hard to please.

I am not sure
I will pick up the cues,
understand the humor,
Be "in,"
Be "part of,"
Be "with it,"
in the new neighborhood,
at the new job,
with the new friends.

Natasha Josefowitz, Ph.D., is a professor of management at the College of Business Administration, San Diego State University, where she has developed a course for women in management. Her book *Paths to Power,* a woman's guide from first job to top executive, has been named Business Book of Outstanding Merit. Her articles have appeared in the *Harvard Business Review, Psychology Today,* and *Ms.* Magazine, among others.

Dr. Josefowitz designs and runs programs for executives, supervisors, homemakers returning to work, and students on topics dealing with management skills, upward mobility, and male/female dynamics at work. She is a well-known lecturer, speaking for professional women's groups and national management associations, and is a frequent guest on radio and television talk shows.

Françoise Gilot is well known as a painter, illustrator, and author. Her lithographs illustrate *Pouvoir Tout Dire,* a book of poems by Paul Eluard, and she is both the poet and illustrator of *The Fugitive Eye. Life with Picasso,* which she wrote with Carlton Lake, was a Book-of-the-Month Club selection, and *Le Regard et Son Masque,* soon to appear in its translation, *Interface: The Painter and His Mask,* are important contributions to the understanding of art and the artist. Ms. Gilot is married to Dr. Jonas Salk.